Diabolo:

The yo-yo set free

by **Dan Roddick** for Jester Games

Illustrated by **Mike Daley**

Produced by **Christian Ruiz**

The Diabolo: The yo-yo set free

ISBN 0-9677972-0-9

Printed in the United States of America by
KNI Press, Inc., Anaheim, CA

Book and cover design and photography by
Dan Roddick

Contents

Introduction: Get ready to be amazed

In fact, if we were to make a list of truly amazing things, the diabolo would certainly be on it. What makes it so amazing? Well, remember that to be amazed is to be over-whelmed with wonder. To be astounded, stunned and astonished. Or even to be dumfounded, confused and bewildered. All this from a simple toy? Yes, this and much, much more. As you become acquainted with your diabolo, you will definitely experience all of these feelings. Usually we are amazed when things happen that we don't expect. Show your diabolo to people who have never seen one before and ask them to tell you how they think it works. It takes a pretty clever person to imagine even some of the possibilities. They may think that it looks a bit like a yo-yo, but it's not attached to the string. And what about those sticks? When you begin to show someone how it spins, it's as if you are doing some sort of magic, and in fact, it is a magical device. As it is with any good magician, the audience will be amazed.

Being able to amaze people (including yourself) is only part of the fun. The diabolo has a lot of other features going for it too. Obviously, it's easily portable. No problem carrying it along in a backpack or on your bike rack. Almost anywhere is a good place to play. The park is great, but the living room will work fine also as long as you don't have too many breakable items scattered around. Even the beach or pool works great. The diabolo can handle sand and water just fine. If it falls and gets wet and sandy, just spin it up again. It's self cleaning! The diabolo is also relatively inexpensive compared to a lot of other games and hobbies. Top fuel drag racing, for instance, can get very pricey. Even something as simple as tennis or golf can add up as you keep buying new balls and paying fees to play. As a diabolo player, all that you'll have to do is occasionally replace the string. The diabolo itself is almost indestructible and requires no real maintenance. Sure, the yo-yo is inexpensive and compact also. But, trust us on this, if you like the yo-yo, you're going to love the diabolo. They both involve a spinning thing and a string, but that's where the diabolo truly takes off. Because it can fly, free of the string, infinite new possibilities are open. A single player can perform not only the string tricks of a yo-yo, but also the tossing and catching tricks of a juggler. With more than one player, the game gets really hot with throws and catches that are more like playing with a flying disc. Because of the arm motion, throwing and movement, diabolo play is also good exercise. Even at the end of a solo session, you'll be amazed at how much of a workout your arms will get; just another benefit of this simple toy.

History: A new old fad

As inventions go, the diabolo has to be one of the more impressive achievements. Now, admittedly, the invention of the wheel was a big deal, but let's face it, the wheel was a lot easier to figure out than the diabolo. As you'll see, most people have a hard time figuring out the diabolo even after they've seen it. This is a thing of genius. Now just who was the genius who dreamed up the diabolo? Well, that's a tough one. Like the wheel, we don't have the name of our genius inventor. Every school kid knows that Eli Whitney invented the cotton gin and that Alex Bell invented the telephone, but those guys came up with their bright ideas a little over a hundred years ago. There are historians who think that the diabolo has been spinning in China for over 4,000 years! Nobody has a complete history of the diabolo's popularity over all of that time, but it seems pretty certain that it has become a fad over and over again. It has certainly achieved that level of popularity several times in Europe.

Are you wondering about the name diabolo? Apparently the Chinese name for the toy was and is "kouen gen" which means something like "hollow whistling bamboo." This makes sense. Many Chinese diabolos have been made from hollow bamboo and have been designed to whistle when they spin rapidly. The term diabolo was probably introduced by European enthusiasts and it dosen't a refer to Satan, but comes from a Greek word, meaning "to throw across."

How it Works: A physics course on a string

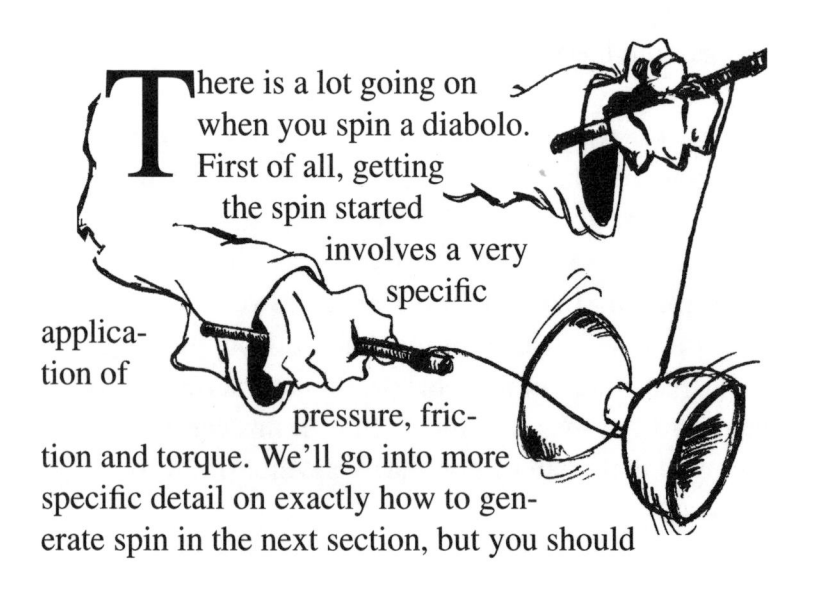

There is a lot going on when you spin a diabolo. First of all, getting the spin started involves a very specific application of pressure, friction and torque. We'll go into more specific detail on exactly how to generate spin in the next section, but you should know that the process relies on several laws of physics all working in tandem to produce the impressive spin. A yo-yo begins to spin for a very different reason. It is simply rolling down its string. The diabolo, however, is merely poised on its string. To get it to spin, you must apply a series of pulls to get it moving. If your pulling motion is symmetrical the diabolo will never begin to spin. The pulls on one side must be exaggerated while the pulls on the other side are minimized. Once the diabolo is spinning, lots of cool scientific things begin to come into play. The diabolo tends to stay in its position because the spin generates what is known as "gyroscopic stability." As the name implies, it's the same phenomenon that keeps a gyroscope, or a top, upright. When either a top or a gyroscope stops spinning it will fall over. Likewise, a diabolo that is not spinning has no stability. A rapidly-spinning and well-balanced diabolo wants to stay in the same position that it is currently spinning. That is, it resists turning around its axis or center. This tendency is the key to many diabolo tricks. It also can be a problem for you if you want to change the position of the spinning toy. Making those changes, without killing the spin requires that you take into account even more of the characteristics of spinning bodies. For instance, when you want to change the angle of the spinning diabolo, you won't be able to simply push it where you want it to go. Because of something called the "precession effect," the result of your pushing motion on the spinning diabolo will actually be 90 degrees "off" of the effect that you would expect if you gave a similar push to a diabolo that was suspended, but not spinning. You got all that? If not, don't worry about it. All the tricks and maneuvers are designed to achieve all of these seemingly complex effects. Many times the moves themselves will be very simple. It's a lot like the rest of your life; even if you don't know why it's all happening, you can still have a good time.

What Have We Got Here?

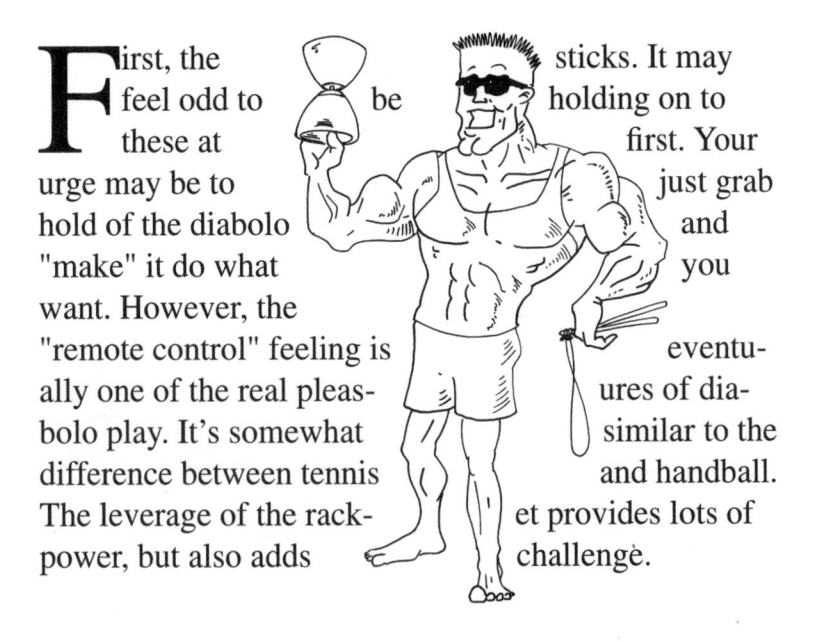

First, the sticks. It may feel odd to be holding on to these at first. Your urge may be to just grab hold of the diabolo and "make" it do what you want. However, the "remote control" feeling is eventually one of the real pleasures of diabolo play. It's somewhat similar to the difference between tennis and handball. The leverage of the racket provides lots of power, but also adds challenge.

Likewise, the leverage of these juggling tools will give you some amazing power when you eventually figure out what you're doing. These sticks are sometimes made of wood, but assuming that you have a Jester Games diabolo, yours are constructed of the same space age polymer that NASA uses in the space shuttle...plastic. They should never break unless you are trying some tricks that are too dangerous for this book. Most players hold the sticks near the end away from the string, but occasionally you may want to choke up on them a bit. Some of our younger spinners find that they have better control by moving their hands up a bit toward the string end. The most important thing is for the grip and motion to feel comfortable.

See the illustration below for the correct method of tying the string. It was probably already tied onto the sticks when you got them, but it's good to know how to tie it on when you eventually have to replace the string.

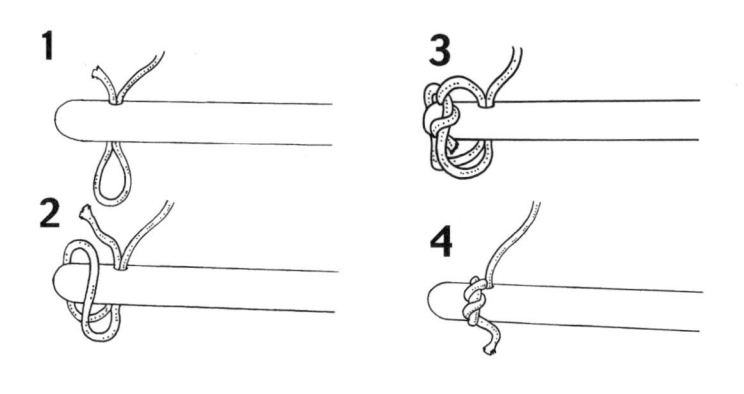

By that time, incidentally, you have our guarantee that you'll be pretty darn hot with the diabolo. It takes a good bit of play to wear out a string.

Now, how long should the string be? Well, that's a good question that cannot be easily answered because, as they say, "It depends." First of all, it depends on how big you are. Obviously, those smaller players who are choking up on the sticks are also going to need a shorter string because their arms are not long and not far apart. Also, they're not far above the floor.

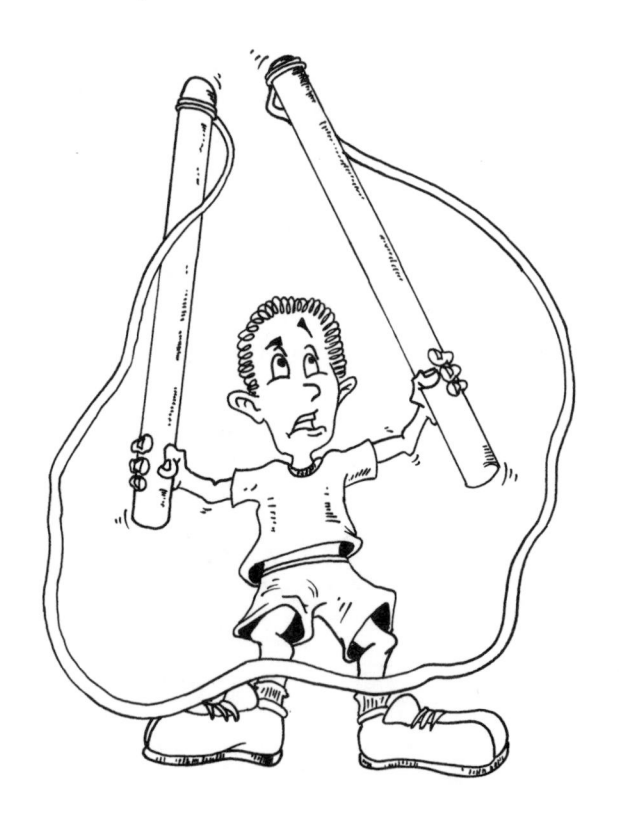

An old rule of thumb used to be that the string should be as long as the distance from your nose to the ground. Well, for some tricks that you eventually will be doing that length will be fine, but to start off, we suggest that you go a good bit shorter. Try a string that is about the distance from your belly button to the ground.

Do remember that it's easy to adjust your string length by simply looping another loop of string over the tip of the stick where it's tied. Just make a simple overhand knot and slip it over the end of the stick. Just one more loop over each stick end will shorten your string by about 4 inches which is a big difference that you will easily be able to feel.

The string that came with your Jester Games diabolo is made of the same materials that NASA uses in their space suits...cotton and nylon. If you end up replacing it yourself you may want to experiment with different blends and thicknesses. It's really a matter of personal taste. Some players swear that very thin string works better while others are equally certain that the opposite is true. Fortunately, it's pretty simple and inexpensive to determine what you like best. Knock yourself out and try every new kind of string that you come across.

And now (drum roll) finally, the star of the whole show. No, not you... that may come later. We're talking about the the diabolo. As we've already told you, the modern diabolo is a scientific marvel. Made of, you guessed it, the very same materials that NASA uses in their billion-dollar space probes...rubber, plastic and steel. The rubber in the Jester Games diabolo is a special blend however that NASA would like to use, but we haven't worked out a deal with them yet. It's just soft enough to not hurt too much if you bonk your head with it, but it's also got what is called great "memory." That allows the diabolo to hit your head and flex, but still remember its shape so it is ready to spin again without being distorted. When something spins as fast as the diabolo, very small imperfections can create really significant imbalances. Just watch a ceiling fan that is not symmetrical and you'll see as it begins to turn faster it will develop a speed wobble that could rip it out of the ceiling if it goes too fast. Well, the diabolo

10

goes even faster, so the distribution of weight must be nearly perfect. If it isn't, you'll see a wobble or a gradual turn which is caused by the imbalance. Fortunately, the Jester Games diabolo is balanced in the same way that NASA balances their G-force simulator...trial and error. We just kept building them until we found a method that was nearly perfect. If you look closely, you'll see that your Jester Games diabolo is actually made of nine parts. So how do we perfectly balance nine parts? Seems like an even number would be easier doesn't it? Well, the trick is that one part, the axle, is

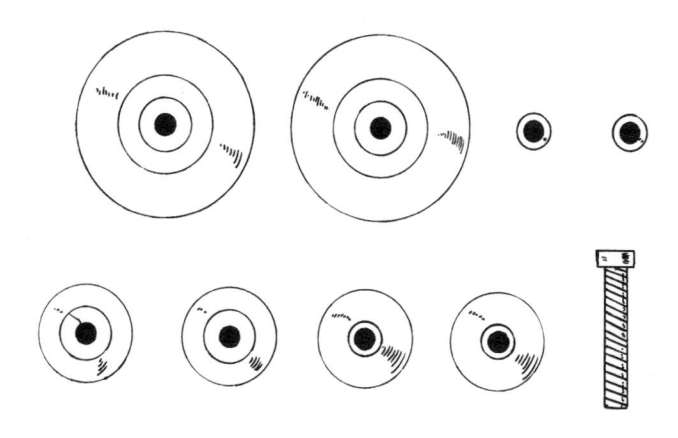

dead center in the middle. If you're pretty good at remembering how things go back together, feel free to take it apart. Bet they didn't tell you to do that with your Game Boy computer, did they? Just twist the end in your left hand clockwise and the nut will spin off. Count the parts and spin it back together.

If you can't figure out how to do the reassembly, you really aren't a mechanical person are you? Mail it back to Jester Games and we'll have one of our reassembly experts restore your diabolo to its original condition at no charge. Alternatively, for quicker service, let any ten- year old kid in the neighborhood do it for you. This is a good thing to see because sometime you may hear a loose rattle in your diabolo and the nut may need to be tightened up a bit. It doesn't need to be screaming tight, just so it feels firm and solid.

Remember this is a space-age item that you have here. The traditional diabolos were made of bamboo or wood. Much more fragile and difficult to balance. Better living through chemistry and all that stuff. The axle is a very smooth piece of aluminum that makes it very easy to get the diabolo really spinning. If you wear that part out, you will be a very, very hot diabolo player. Jester Games will cheerfully replace any axle that you burn out, and sign you up for the demonstration team.

Getting Started: The spin's the thing

Enough talk. Let's get rolling. The spin is the thing, so we need to get some of that going first off. Without spin, the diabolo's like a bird without feathers. Like a toaster with no cord. Like a hot fudge sundae when you're out of ice cream. Like...not worth much at all. It's the spin that makes all the magic. In the beginning we just want to get a little spin going. But first, we need to decide what kind of spinner you're going to be. There's two kinds. There are lefties and there are righties. Quick, throw the book up into the air!

Glad you found your place again. When the book came down, which hand did you catch it in? That will be the hand we'll start with. Now, we'll tell you the truth here. Lots of diabolo players who have been around a long time can only spin it in one direction. That will not be true for you. You're part of the new generatlon of spinners who will fear no rotational direction. You will see, grasshopper, this all will come to pass.

To get things rolling easily, most players begin with a roll start. As promised, we'll assume that you caught the book in your right hand, so we'll start you off as a

13

right-handed spinner (for now).To make things more clear, we'll show the accelerating stick as black..

Place your diabolo on the string and lower it to the floor, off to your right side. A smooth surface is best. If you're outside, bumpy grass may not work well.

Lower your right stick and then drag the diabolo smoothly to your left. See how it rolls? That's what we want. Set it up and try it a few times to smooth out the motion. To get the best spin, pull it as far as you can before you lift the sticks and pick it up. You can even take a step or so in the direction of the roll, but be sure to have the roll be straight and smooth. A common mistake is to roll the diabolo in the correct direction and then roll it back before picking it up. This, of course, gets things started with the wrong spin.

Pick it up smoothly, without jerking the diabolo which

Be Bispingual!

Learn to do both spins as you go along. Why learn both you ask when one seems to be hard enough? Well, because there are so many cool things that you will want to be doing soon that are much easier if you can handle either spin. The reason to start learning it now is that if you become too comfortable with only your "native" spin over a long period of time, it will be more difficult to learn the other. So, even from the beginning, when you're working on a move with one spin, switch it over and try it on the other. Another benefit of doing this is that you will be able to rest your native spinning arm. Despite this, for simplicity, we'll be describing the techniques in this book from the perspective of right-handed spinners. You lefties are reputed to be more creative, so you can translate for yourselves.

can disrupt the spin. Once you've lifted it up, you'll see that you already have a pretty good spin going.

A Teaching Tip

If you're already pretty good at spinning the diabolo and you want to give a friend a quick start on how it feels to work with a lot of spin, just spin your diabolo up and then transfer it to him or her by lowering it on to their string.

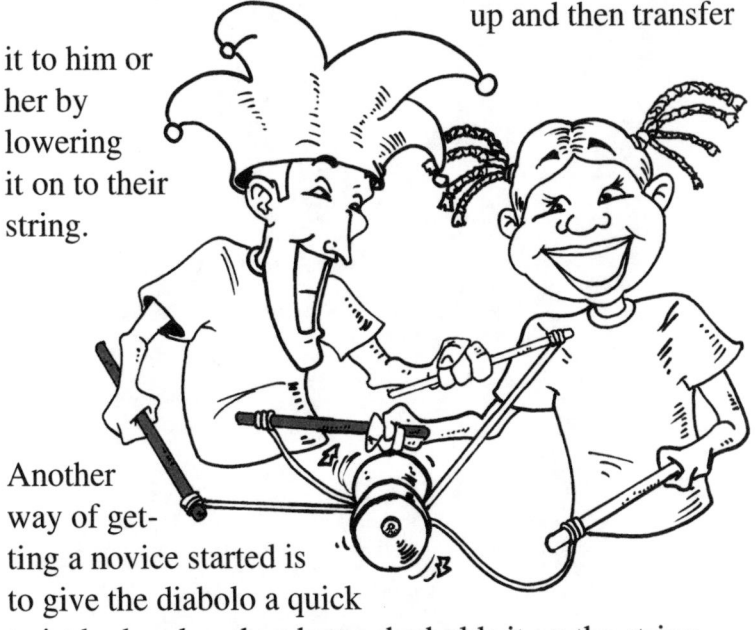

Another way of getting a novice started is to give the diabolo a quick twist by hand as they he or she holds it on the string.

Both these techniques help make very early attempts a bit easier, but obviously everyone should learn how to get their own spin started. We just want to make those first attempts as be encouraging as possible by giving our newbie a good feel of the spin.

Tap, tap, tapping

OK, so it's spinning on the string. Just watch it for a moment. If your roll on the floor was smooth and straight, the spin should last for about three seconds before it stops. The trick now is to keep it going. Your natural tendency may be to start lifting on both sticks. Try that for a while. How's it going? Not too well probably because in order to generate the spin we need to maximize the pull on the right side and minimize it on the left. We can do that in several ways, but the most basic is what we call a "tapping" motion. Just imagine that you're tapping a drum with your right stick. What's the left stick doing? Pretty much nothing. You'll notice the tip of the left stick goes up and down a little just to take up the slack of the string, but you don't have to do that. It will just happen naturally. So how fast should you be tapping? Well, let's look at a couple of different styles, both of which work well once you learn them. First try the slow tap. That's about two taps per second. With the slow pace, you'll see that the diabolo moves up and down with each tap. Then, speed your pace up as fast as you can go with very short, crisp motions. At about six taps per second, the diabolo will hardly move up and down at all. Experiment and see what feels most comfortable for you. One key thing to remember is that your tapping strokes should be up and down, not side-to-side. Any side-to-side motion reduces the effectiveness of your technique. Test your efficiency by spinning the diabolo up as fast as you can and then stopping to see how long it spins on the string. You should be able to get to 8 to 10 seconds of spin after a bit of practice.

Problems?

 So as your tapping up your spin, you probably have discovered some "problems." Well, they aren't really problems, you know, but rather opportunities. This is your opportunity to learn how to control the "attitude" of your diabolo. In this case a bad attitude is when the diabolo begins to tip or turn. If it tips or turns too far it will fall off of your string. Let's deal with tipping first. As you're tapping, you may notice that the diabolo begins to move away from being level with the ground. This is called tipping. It comes in two flavors. Either the cup of the diabolo which is facing away from you is higher than it should be, or the cup facing you is too high.

The tipping fix

One general technique fixes either situation. Think of your tapping stick as the tipping control. To fix tipping, as you continue to tap, move the tapping stick (right for righties) toward the end of the diabolo that is too high. Easy to remember, right? Move the tapping stick toward the high end. Don't be afraid to slide it out there. Here(looking from above) is a right-handed accelerator pulling his stick back to lower the end of the diabolo that is facing him.

When you're just beginning, keep your eye on the diabolo and nip tipping in the bud. As soon as you see any tilt, shove or pull that tapping stick to fix it before you're tipping out of control. As you gain experience, this adjustment will become second nature and you won't even think about it, but when you're starting out, it's best to pay very close attention.
-Don't be afraid to overreact. That's how you see the power of your controls. Then you can dial it back to what you need.
-Even though movement of the tapping stick is the key

19

to remembering how to fix tipping, you can also use some movement of the other stick to smooth out your adjustment. As you push the tipping stick forward, it will feel natural to slide the other stick back a bit to add to the adjustment effect.

-No matter what adjustment that you make...keep tapping. Spin is your friend.

Turning

Just like two troublesome cousins whose visits are not really welcome, turning is closely related to tipping. Turning occurs when the diabolo begins to angle to your left or your right. Later we'll talk about how to fix this problem, but for now just go along. That is, if the diabolo is turning, move your feet to keep the closer cup pointing directly toward you. This keeps everything squared up. It's not as if you have an audience yet or that you have to place the diabolo at a particular angle for your partner, so for now just go with the flow and keep moving if you have to. It's good exercise.

Orbits: Loop-de-loop

Now that you've got things spinning, let's take it out for a ride. These moves may remind you of yo-yo tricks that you have seen. They are similar because the diabolo never leaves the string.

Front

First, get your best spin going. Then, swing the diabolo up to your right side overhead and down on the left. That big circle or orbit will bring you back down to the bottom, but you'll notice that

something is different. Your strings are crossed! To uncross them, do the reverse orbit.
The key to this move is a good spin and smooth orbiting. Do be careful to make sure that there are no breakables in your orbit area and also be sure not to hit yourself on the head.

With a Turn

If you're very observant, you may have figured out that you can keep the strings from crossing if you turn with the diabolo as you orbit. Give that a try too.

Sides

You can also do a variations of the orbit that take them around your left or right side.

Or...Around Your Back

Inside

The inside orbit requires a leap of faith.

Be a bit careful unless you want some free plastic surgery on your nose. First, check to make sure that your string is short enough so that you can swing the diabolo in toward you while you hold your arms straight out in front. To set up the move, step around to the right side of the spinning diabolo, then orbit it out away from you and up and back toward your body. That's where the string being short enough comes in.

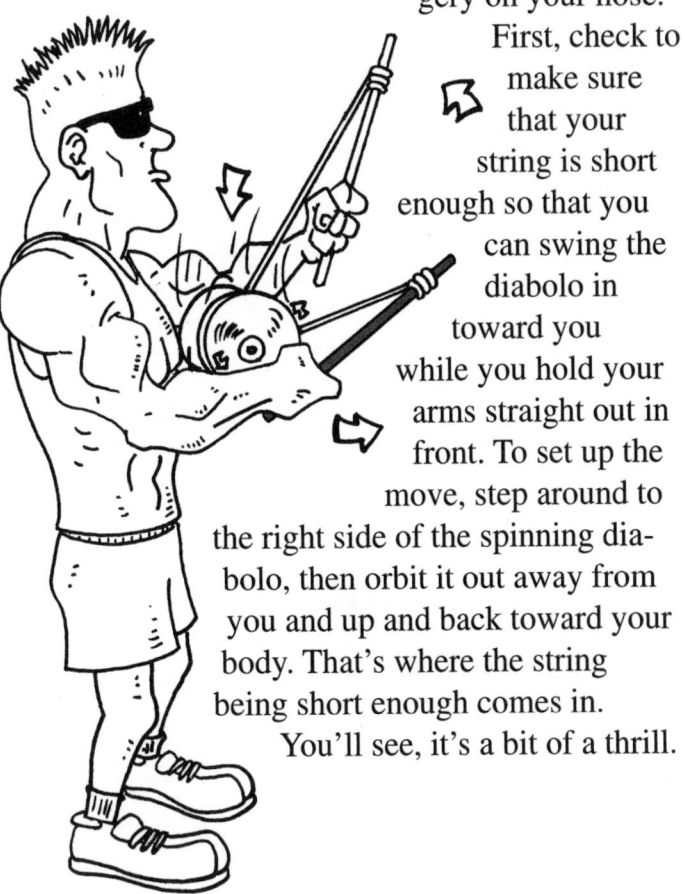

You'll see, it's a bit of a thrill.

Launches: Set it free

ere's where we start to leave the yo-yo in the
dust. It's time to get some air!

Front

Before you launch one, you don't really have to have
the diabolo spinning at very top speed, but it is very
important to make sure that you don't have any tilting
at all and that you are perfectly squared up (no turning
should be going on at the time). Of course,
you do need a certain amount of spin
just to stabilize the flight, but being at
dead level is critical. When you try the
first launch, don't go very high. Up to
eye level will be fine.

To initiate the launch, go through these
steps:

-Spin up
-Square up
-Check level, then...

-Lift and spread your sticks to "catapult" the diabolo straight up

If it catches on the string or doesn't go up cleanly, you may have had the diabolo slightly off level or have not lifted straight up. Most likely, it will go up nicely and you will be pleased and proud.

Catching

Your moment of Zen can be short lived if you're not prepared to catch what you've thrown. The catching process can sometimes be tricky and frustrating. This can be especially true if you're generally pretty good at catching things. It can feel like that superior eye-hand coordination that you were always able to count on has checked out without notice.

Toss...drop. Toss...drop. Toss...drop. Come on now. This can't be that hard! Toss...drop. Well, a couple of things may be causing you to star in this dropfest:

-One of the most common mistakes is to try to catch with the sticks too close together. Somehow, we want to catch it with the sticks. The " Mr. Miyaghi" syndrome, we call it. Like trying to catch a fly with a pair of chopsticks. Remember...from *The Karate Kid*? If not, rent it tonight.

The main point is that you want to catch with the string, not the sticks. Therefore, you need to have the sticks be far enough apart to make the string be pretty taut. This is mainly so you can line it up more easily. It's very important to make sure that the line of the string is perpendicular to the diabolo. Without the string taut, that line can hard to determine.

The second common error is to try to catch the diabolo in the middle of the string. After you've caught a good many, you'll be able to do that pretty consistently, but for now, don't try that at home or elsewhere!

It's surprisingly difficult to judge how far out to put the sticks when you try to catch in the middle. Maybe it's because you're accustomed to catching with your hands. Who knows? The trick is to catch much closer to your tapping stick. In fact, as the diabolo is coming down, you basically point the tapping stick right at the axle of the diabolo. That makes the tapping stick be higher, and that's a good thing also. Keep the other stick lower, and be sure to keep the string fairly taut and perpendicular to the diabolo. When the diabolo lands, it will slide down the string.

As it does that, you'll need to raise your non-tapping stick to help the diabolo to settle down in the middle of your string. And...you'll be happily tapping again with the diabolo safely back home.

Learning to Learn

If you're just starting and you've read this far at one
sitting, put down the book and play! You cannot learn
something like this all at once.
In fact, there's no reason to
learn it very quickly unless
you've made some sort of "....bet
I can learn to do this in X amount
of time" wagers. Learning to do
such things is the real fun. Now,
don't misunderstand. Taking up the
challenge of something that can
only be achieved through diligent
practice and study is a
magnificent thing.
We're just saying that
there is no particular
need to rush this
process. Of course,
there is great satisfac-
tion in being able to do
something that you once thought
that you would never master. In fact, the thrill of hitting
a move for the first time, no matter how clumsily, is a
hard feeling to match. Actually, even if you do have
that bet and need to learn really quickly, you'll probably find that a slower pace ends up being more effec-

tive. This is complex stuff. Your brain and body need some time to process it all. You'll be amazed at how often you'll stumped on a move, but if you take a break and return an hour later, your body has somehow learned how to do it. This challenge continues, no matter how good you become. When the jesters at Jester Games are learning new tricks, we like to keep the diabolo around the house and office. Then, every time we pass by, or take a break from something else, we'll give the new move another try. It works, and it does wonders for the rest of the day too. This is a journey that we're on, not a destination. Don't ever press so hard on it that you get frustrated in an unpleasant way. Life has enough frustrations as it is. Why add any more?

Throughout this book you will find three proficiency levels described, with the tests designed to measure your skills. If you wish, you can submit your test results and get official Jester Games certification of your skill level. This is particularly useful if you don't know any other diabolo players. Sometimes it's nice to get an objective idea of how you are progressing. However, it's time to start finding some other people to learn to play because you'll need some friends for the cooperative and competitive play that comes up later in the book. Just go out to your local park and practice a while. You'll find some new friends, guaranteed.
But now, for the first proficiency challenge.

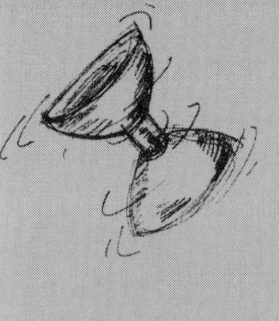

Proficiency Challenge

(Level 1-Spinner)

To achieve the Level 1 (Spinner) Skill Award, the candidate must fulfill the following:

A. Acceleration

Using a roll start and the tapping method of acceleration , the candidate must be able to produce a smooth spin that is rapid enough to last at least 7 seconds after the tapping motion is stopped.

Length of spin- _____seconds

B. Adjustment

To demonstrate the ability to adjust tilt and accommodate turning, the candidate must complete three separate periods of at least two minutes of continuous spinning each.

#1Time _____ #2Time_____ #3Time_____

C. Orbits

The candidate must demonstrate each of the following orbits:

Front _____ Back_____ Left _____ Right _____
Front with turn_____ Inside _____
Front with orbit back to unwrap string_____

D. Launching and Catching

The candidate must demonstrate the ability to launch and catch by completing the two requirements that follow:

1. Catch series-Achieve a series of five launches and catches without a drop. Short periods of acceleration (less than 5 seconds) may occur between the launches.
_____

2. Time Launch- Achieve three successful launches and catches in which the air time is at least 4 seconds each.

Launch #1 Time_____ Launch #2 Time_____
Launch #3 Time_____

The candidate may make as many attempts at each requirement as he or she desires, however, the entire challenge must be completed within a 30 minute period. The test must be verified by two adult individuals who serve as examiners and timers. The examiners should initial each result and sign and date the completed application for certification.

Jester Games Diabolo Spinner Skill Award

Name_____

Address_____

        _____

        _____

Phone_____

E-mail_____

Has qualified in all the requirements for the Spinner
level of diabolo play as attested by:

_____

_____

This _____ day of _____, 19__

Photocopy this form and mail the completed form and
a $ 12 check or money order (payable to Jester Games)
to:

Jester Games
4924 Balboa #415
Encino, CA 91316
jestergames@hotmail.com

Certified players will receive a Jester Games Diabolo
Spinner Proficiency Certificate and a Jester Games
shirt.
Please allow 3 weeks for processing and mailing.

34

Hyperspinning

By now you should have the tapping method of acceleration down pretty well. It works fine for many tricks, but in which we'll really want to make the diabolo sing. Welcome to the world of hyperspinning! One of the first techniques to try is:

Crosswhipping

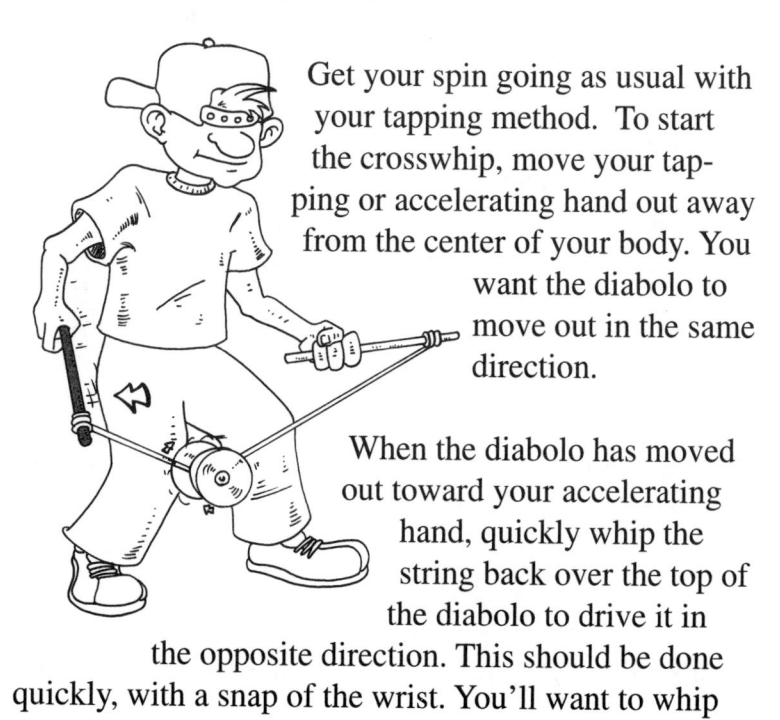

Get your spin going as usual with your tapping method. To start the crosswhip, move your tapping or accelerating hand out away from the center of your body. You want the diabolo to move out in the same direction.

When the diabolo has moved out toward your accelerating hand, quickly whip the string back over the top of the diabolo to drive it in the opposite direction. This should be done quickly, with a snap of the wrist. You'll want to whip

35

the stick back past the other stick to get a full motion. In order to do that you'll have to make the whipping motion be either over and in front of your other stick or under and behind it. Otherwise, your sticks will collide and the diabolo will probably be thrown free of the string.

Try this a number of times, but don't try to keep it going yet. Just spin as you normally would and then periodically give a single pull out and whip. Even that should start to add some additional spin. Keep doing these occasional whips until you start to feel like you have good control of the diabolo and that you're able to have each whipping motion add a significant amount of additional spin.

The next step is to begin to link these whipping motions together. What we're really aiming for is a continuing motion of crosswhipping that allows you to add a great deal of spin. Begin by trying to do two, three or more whips in a row. At this point, you might find that you're having some problems again with tilting. This is one of the cool things about crosswhipping. You can easily fix any tilting problems as you go. If the diabolo is tilting away from you (nose down), have your whipping motion go above and in front of your other stick. A few of those motions should correct the tilt. You say that it's tilting back toward you now (tail down)? You guessed it. Now the fix is to switch your whipping motions to below and behind the other stick.

You'll notice in the illustrations of crosswhipping that the players are pointing their sticks down toward the diabolo. This angle sometimes seems to make it easier to make a smooth change between the over and under motions. So, you might ask, "If the over motion tilts it back and the under motion tilts in forward, how will I manage to keep it level?" Well, it's a little like steering a car. You don't just freeze the steering wheel in place. It's that you make a series of adjustments that (hopefully) keep you on the road. As you get the feel for crosswhipping, you'll begin to automatically adjust the mix of over and under motions to keep the diabolo level. When it's really singing, you may find yourself doing every other stroke over and under or two over and two under. Whatever works for you.

Speaking of making the diabolo sing, when you begin to link the whipping motions together, you'll find that the non-whipping stick begins to get into the action also. In fact, you'll find that you move it almost as much as the whipping stick in order to keep control of the string and the diabolo. The resulting double motion is full-fledged cross-

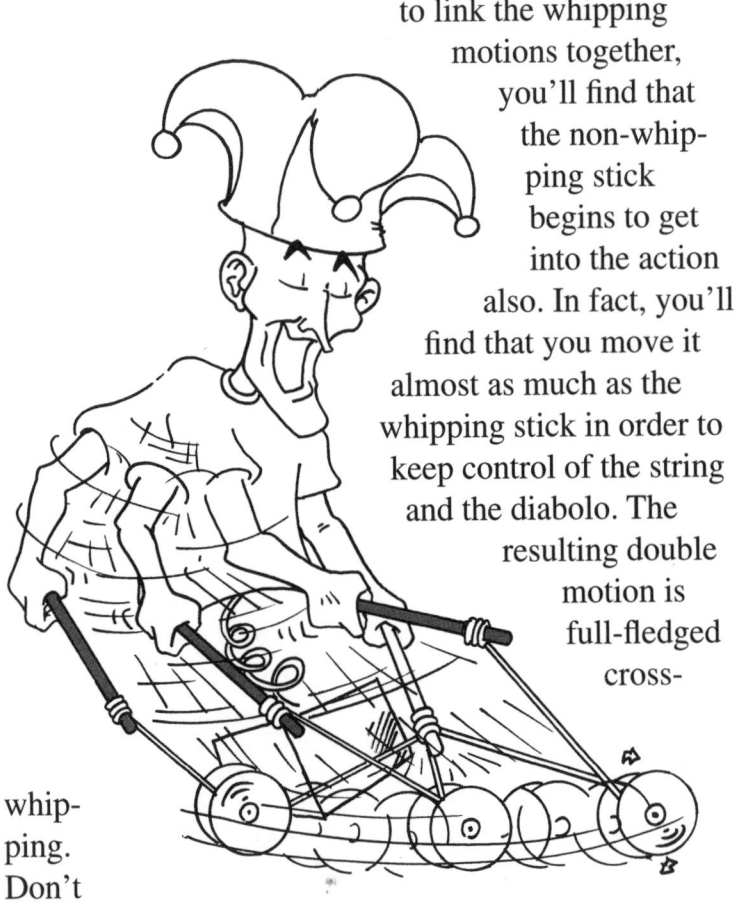

whipping. Don't worry if it doesn't all happen at once. It will all start to come together with practice.

Circles: Round and round

We call this family of tricks the "circles" because it appears that the diabolo is circling around a point. These moves are really little, controlled launches which you quickly catch on the other end of your string. The easiest way to get a feel for how it works is to start by doing some circles without going around anything. Try doing a low launch off of your non-accelerating side which you catch on the opposite side. Do just one at first to get the feel, but the key is to do a series of the launches. When you do that you'll see that the motion of the diabolo begins to describe a circle as it slides down the string and back to your non-accelerating side.

One leg

Once you have the feel for a front circle, try working around your leg. Begin by stepping through the string with the leg on your non-accelerating side. If you have good balance, it probably will be easier at first to do the circles if you don't put your foot down. This will make it easier to adjust your position to the diabolo.

Don't think that the diabolo will automatically do circles for you. It does look like that when a top player does it, but especially in the beginning, you'll have to be really paying attention to keep catching and launching the diabolo. As you get better, you'll be able to make the subtle adjustments that you need to do a series of many smooth circles without stopping. Four or five in a row are usually enough to wow most spectators. Remember that smoothness and symmetry are what makes the circle series really impressive.

Both sides

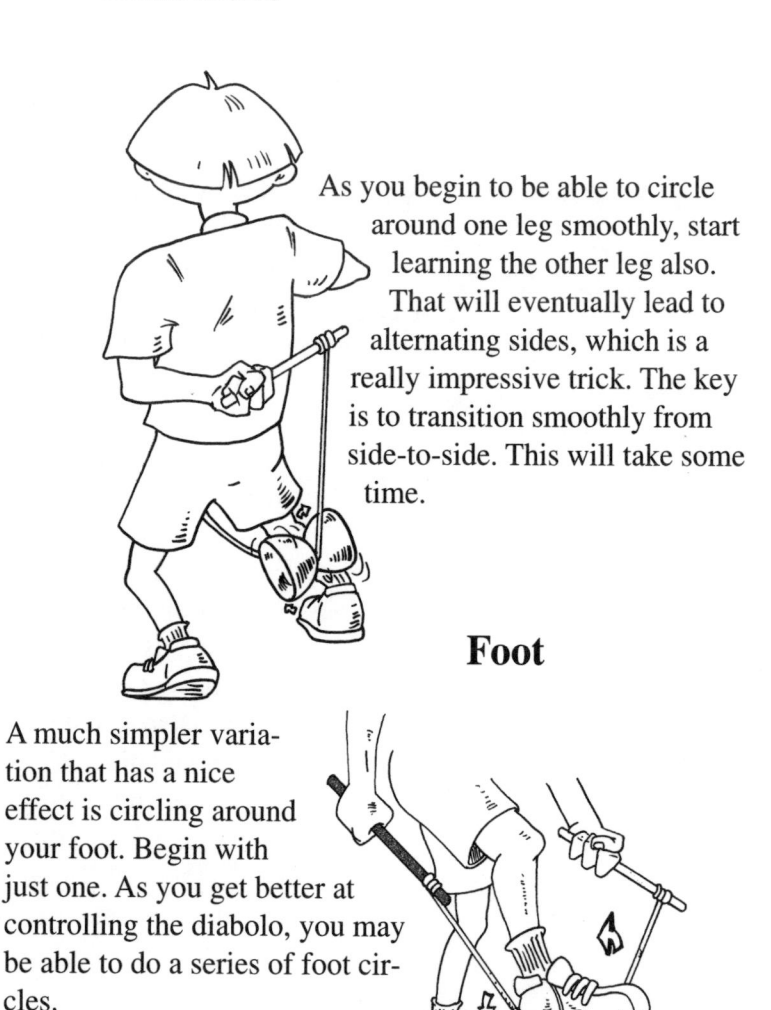

As you begin to be able to circle around one leg smoothly, start learning the other leg also. That will eventually lead to alternating sides, which is a really impressive trick. The key is to transition smoothly from side-to-side. This will take some time.

Foot

A much simpler variation that has a nice effect is circling around your foot. Begin with just one. As you get better at controlling the diabolo, you may be able to do a series of foot circles.

41

One arm

Now we're getting to the really fancy stuff. When you start doing these moves, be sure that you have your hat out for the money from the admiring crowd. It also starts to get a little risky here because you can easily pop yourself in the nose if you're not careful. The diabolo will be circling around the upper part of your accelerating arm. For righties, point the right stick to your right as you bend your elbow. Keep the left stick high because it will control the circling diabolo. The weight of the diabolo will carry it under your arm. To do more than one, pay close attention to keeping the circle in the same plane.

Jumps

A really great variation on your circle move is the jump. You can use it on almost every circle position and often you can go directly into it after you have established the circle. Instead of having the diabolo go smoothly under your leg, foot or arm, have it jump over to the other side of the string instead. You'll see that the motion is quite different than the one you used for the circles. Timing is...well, it's everything.

These jumps have to be done to a pretty quick tempo or you'll be back doing circles again. When you combine the circles and the jumps you'll find the combination of the two different tempos to be entertaining (and challenging).

Here's a real crowd-pleasing jump move. Wrap the string around the back of your neck and jump the diabolo from side-to-side. We suggest that you have the diabolo spinning away from your face for this trick. You'll find it helpful to slide the string back and forth with each jump.

Advanced
Launches and Catches: get hot!

Let's face it. Big time launches are the real "ooh...ah" of diabolo play. That's where we really separate ourselves from the yo-yo and other jugglers. Flinging up a monster launch which you catch smoothly is a real rush. Don't waste that air time though. There's lots to be done.

Launch and spin

Of course if it's a bad launch, your time will be spent chasing it down. Do not launch wildly when you're around others. That's a great way to lose friends and good places to play. Launch only what can be caught. When you see a nice

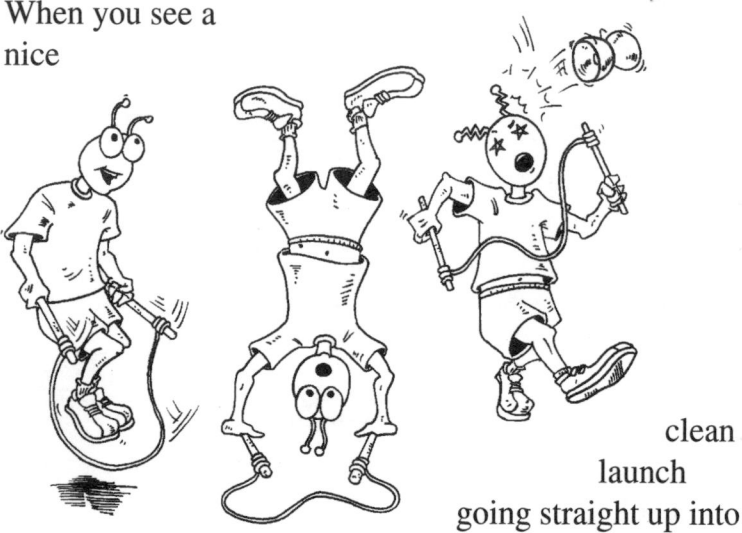

clean launch going straight up into the stratosphere you might want to use the time until it returns. Use your sticks and string as a jump rope. Three jumps is pretty good. Four are sensational and five, well...let us know when you do five. You can also mix in some spins and cartwheels while you're at it. Just don't lose track of the diabolo, which is definitely coming down. Two rope jumps, a cartwheel and a spin followed by a diabolo bonk on the noggin can be kind of embarrassing.

Cross-armed catch

This catch doesn't require a big launch, just enough time to get your arms switched. In fact, it can look even cooler if you don't have much time to make the switch. Do a normal launch, just over your head. Then, cross your arms and stretch the string out for the catch. In this case it's probably easier to catch in the middle of the string so you can bounce the diabolo up right away into another launch. Then, switch your arms back for the catch. Now, the really hot set up is to do one cross-armed catch and then catch the next launch with the opposite cross-armed catch. You'll have to be quick (and flexible) to pull this off, but it's really a nice series of moves. When you master this you should be able to do several of these cross-armed switches in a row.

Behind-the-back

Some catches are challenging because they have to be done very precisely and useful because they allow you to go smoothly into another move. The behind-the-back catch is a good example. Make a high launch because you'll need some time to get set up correctly for this catch. While the diabolo is in the air quickly put your arms behind your back by taking the string over your head. You want to catch the dia- bolo on your accelerating side so push that stick away from your body and have the other stick behind your back. Set up to catch the diabolo as it comes down under your accelerating arm. Be sure that the string is lined up with the angle of the diabolo. When the diabolo lands, it should slide smoothly behind your back so you can launch it again from the non-accelerating side. If you can do this again you're really doing a big jump around your whole body. Remember that keeping good alignment is key. To do so you'll have to bend your hips forward to make room for the diabolo to slide from one side to the other.

Trampoline

This is a catch and launch combined into one move.
Put up a pretty high toss and step under it with your
arms raised directly over your head. Remember what
we told you about catching close to the accelerating
stick tip. Well...now forget that. If you've done any
trampoline bouncing at all you know that it's important
to bounce right in the middle.
One big off-center launch and
you're bouncing on the
floor (once). So, line up
directly under the
falling diabolo and
try to have it land
on the dead center
of your taught
string. When it lands,
absorb the impact and
immediately bounce it right
back up again. With a little
practice you will be able to
do lots of these in a row.
How many? Well until you
hear loud applause and
cheering or you run out of
spin, whichever comes first.

Whip catch

This special catch is also one of the most spectacular ending moves. It's also pretty high risk. That is, even when you're pretty good at it, you can't be absolutely certain that you'll hit it every time. But, hey. Life is a risk. Go for it! A fairly high launch is necessary for several reasons. First, it's more exciting to wait a bit for the diabolo to return. Second, it's more impressive if it's screaming down at high speed. Third, and most importantly, you'll need some time to get set up for this catch.

OK, it's up in the air, right? First make sure it's a good toss that you won't have to run to catch. Next, put both sticks in you catching hand. Do you know how to hold chopsticks correctly? Well, great, but this isn't like that. Hold the sticks at the very end, side-by-side in your palm with the back of your hand facing up. Now here's the key to the grip. Have your index finger between the sticks. The sticks should be in the shape of a long "V" with the string ends apart. Before you even try the whip, practice putting the sticks in one hand and setting up the grip quickly. The grip is critical to this move because it sets up the string to correctly capture the diabolo. Now for the real challenge which will take some practice and a pretty good sense of timing. As the diabolo is falling (it's still up in the air, right?) set up your position so that you are beside it, not behind it. That is, you should be looking at the axle and both cups, not the end. All set? In position, with the one-handed V grip ready?

Here's the whip part. When the diabolo gets to your waist or even below if you're really fast, whip the string over the diabolo. The best way to line it up is to point the tip of the stick that is closer to your body directly at the axle. If the grip is correct, the string should go cleanly over the diabolo and it should be captured again and still spinning fast.

At this point, you're either bowing to thunderous applause or you can separate the sticks and be back in the amazement business.

Stick Tricks: Grind it out!

S ure, grinds are hot skating moves, but the diabolo has a few grinds of its own too. The cool thing about a skating grind is that it's so unexpected. You're rolling along and all at once you're sliding down a rail without using the wheels at all. Diabolo grinds have a similar impact in that you do a whole bunch of string tricks with the diabolo flying all over the place and then, like magic, the diabolo appears to be almost perfectly still while poised on one of the sticks. Dramatic...very dramatic!

As with many of the tricks, the grind will require a good bit of trial and error. The first time you try one, the diabolo will almost certainly fly off immediately. Here are a few hints to shorten the trip to becoming a master grinder. Start first with a grind on your accelerating stick. Get some good spin going and then make a low toss that is slightly off to your accelerating side. Step up beside the diabolo as it falls and catch it on your accelerating stick. Whoops! It flew off right? No biggie. Start again. You'll notice that because of its direction of spin, the diabolo quickly rolled up toward your hand. This time adjust for that by pointing the tip of the stick down when you catch it. Whoops! It slid off of the tip because you had the stick pointed down a little too much.

Try again. Remember that the amount of spin affects how much you must angle the stick down. A screaming fast spin will need more down angle to hold steady. Try a few more times until you start to get a feel for the angle. Notice what good exercise you're getting each time you have to chase the diabolo and bend over to pick it up. We told you that there were lots of benefits to the game.

Adjustment

When you start to get the angle of the stick right, you'll notice that you can control the position of the diabolo by very slightly raising or lowering the tip of the stick. When you've gotten to that point, you'll discover the next problem...no, scratch that. You'll discover the next challenge. After the diabolo is on the stick for only a very short time, you'll notice that it will begin to develop an angle which will soon allow it to jump off of the stick if this is not corrected. So, how can we correct it? Well, you already know the answer because it's the same technique that you use to correct tipping problems when the diabolo is on the string. When one cup of the diabolo gets too high you push the accelerating stick forward to change the angle of the string and fix the tipping. Same theory here, but because the diabolo is spinning directly on the stick, you can just change the angle of the stick to counteract the tipping of the diabolo. Now don't forget that you still have to pay attention to the tip-to-hand angle of the stick. That continues keep the diabolo from running off of the stick.

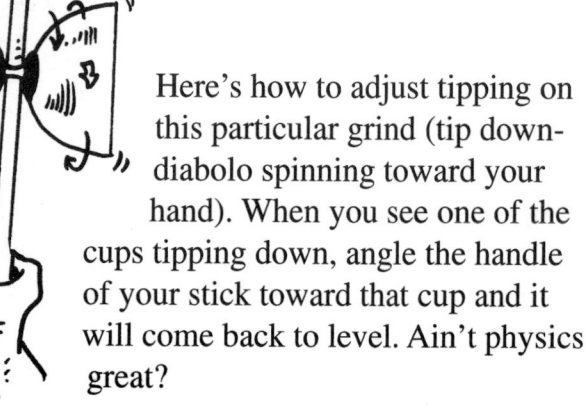

The control for tipping adjustment is side-to-side, not up and down.

Here's how to adjust tipping on this particular grind (tip down-diabolo spinning toward your hand). When you see one of the cups tipping down, angle the handle of your stick toward that cup and it will come back to level. Ain't physics great?

Again when you first try this you'll probably do too much or too little. Stay with it and you will quickly find that the adjustment process starts to become second nature just like adjustment of the diabolo on the string. However, before you get too comfortable try the opposite grind (tip up- diabolo spinning away from you). Just when you thought you were a grinder all of your second nature adjustments are exactly wrong. It's that opposite spin at work. Set this one up like your

first grind, but toss the diabolo a bit to your non-accelerating side and put the stick in on the opposite side of the diabolo. Now, because the diabolo is spinning away from your hand, you'll need to raise the tip up to keep that little rascal

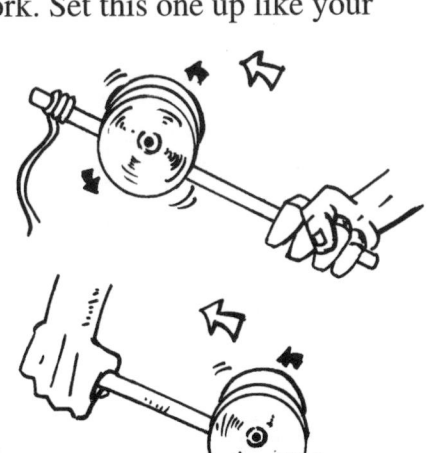

from running away. After you get that under control then you'll find that tipping control is also reversed. Now you'll need to move your hand away from the high side to level out the diabolo. Don't wait too long to try this grind. Somehow it seems to be easier to learn both at about the same time rather than becoming completely comfortable with one variation first.

Oh yeah, we forgot to tell you what to do when you eventually run out of spin. That's the one thing about grinding. Not much chance for acceleration. Keep your eye on the spin and well before it starts to run out, give the diabolo a launch and catch it back on the string to get some more spin. If you launch a little earlier you can actually get a really good launch from a stick grind.

Both hands

Also don't neglect that non-accelerating stick. It will probably not be quite as easy as the other stick, but again, it's best to not get too dependent on just one hand. Start getting comfortable by just switching sticks back and forth on a grind right in front of you.

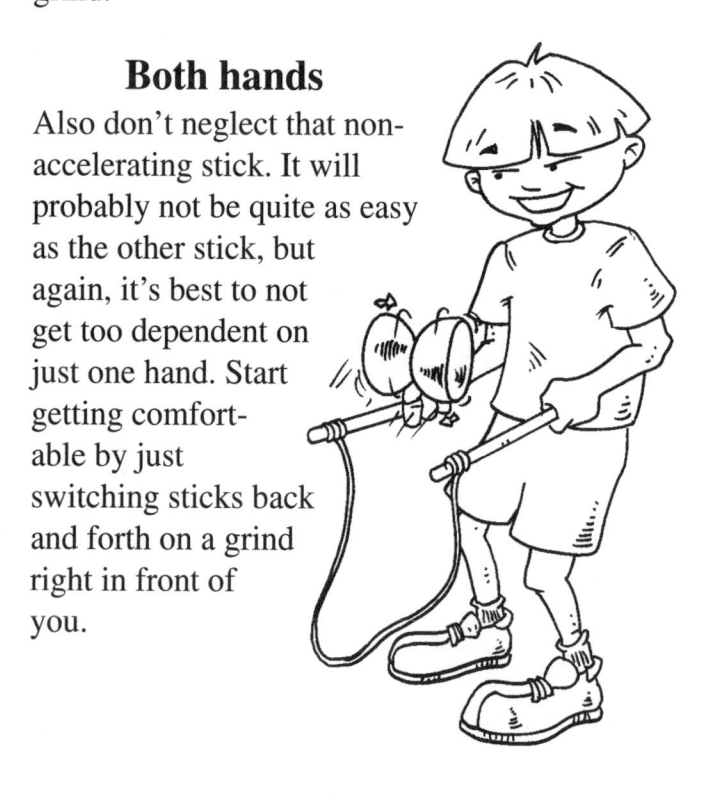

Carries

Think that you're a master grinder by now? Not quite yet. The real test of grind control is carries. First set up your best grind. Then, take it under your leg or behind your back before you launch it up. Get those under control and you're a master!

String Work: A-mazing tricks

Here's all the spider stuff that makes yo-yo so much fun. The diabolo can do it too, and then some.

Elevators

If there is any single trick that is guaranteed to amaze it is the elevator. People love to see you mess with Mr. Gravity's laws. The trick is pretty simple really. First get some mega-spin going. Without a lot of spin, your elevator's going to be stuck in the parking garage. Once you've really got it cooking point your non-accelerating stick across your body at about head level. Lower the accelerating stick. Here comes the trick...

With the lower stick, wrap a loop of the string around the axle and pull down gently.

As the loop tightens up the amazement should begin. The diabolo should rise up the tightened string. This is against gravity my friends. No small feat for a small-time act. Like everything else, you'll have to experiment with the elevator to see how it works best for you. Notice that it makes a difference if you wrap the string over one side of the vertical string or the other. On one side you'll be able to take the elevator all the way to the upper stick and then pop it over top to a normal spinning position. It won't work the other way. Experiment to see which is which. Hey, you have to discover some of this for yourself!

57

Up and down

If you really have a z's on the diabolo you can make the effect of your elevator move even more dramatic. By gently tightening and loosening the loop that you have over the axle you can make the diabolo up and down several times. This trick does take gobs of spin so be prepared for disappointment unless you can really make it sing.

Flipover

This is a good "building block" move for all of the string tricks so we suggest that you work on this one first. Get a good spin going and then swing the diabolo out to the side and over your accelerating stick. When it comes back down you want it to land cleanly on the string between the sticks. If you've kept everything lined up straight the diabolo should continue to spin while suspended by the middle string. Give it a second or so for effect and then flip it back over the accelerating stick and you're back in spinning position. It might take a while to smooth that all out, but once you are able to do it without losing much spin then you're ready to add another flip. When you flip out of the first move just keep the diabolo moving and go right into another flip over the other stick. You need to be smooth and have a good bit of spin to do both flips in a row, but keep at it and it will come around.

Cradle

The cradle trick has a number of variations that you'll discover, but the basic version is a good one to start with because it is easy to understand and it doesn't take a tremendous amount of spin to pull off nicely. It also starts with the flipover. Here are the steps:

1. Do a single flip over your accelerating stick (shown as the dark stick).

2. Push the tip of your non-accelerating stick in under the top string of the flipover.

3. Pull the upper string out with your non-accelerating stick.

Now you have the diabolo trapped.

4. To release it, point the tips of the sticks upward and give the diabolo a small toss straight up.

5. Point the sticks straight up and catch the diabolo on the string cradle.

6. Prepare to be surprised... Dump the tips of the sticks straight down and watch as the string cradle disappears and the diabolo appears on the string in spinning position.

If this worked perfectly for you the first time you tried it you are a truly amazing person who should be spending your time on a challenge more important like world peace or something. For most of us, this series will take many tries before we get all the way to a clean step 6. Success will come from getting more spin and having smoother, faster transitions.

As you begin to work on some of these tricks you'll see that the more complex ones are easier with a greater string length so you may have to get a longer string to pull off some of these challenges.

Eiffel Tower

Ready to do some building with string? Try the Eiffel Tower. Start with your best spin because this takes a while to construct.

1. First grab each string with your fingertips.

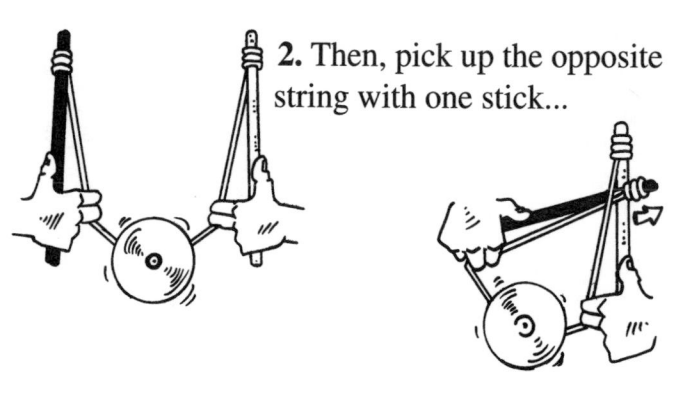

2. Then, pick up the opposite string with one stick...

and spread the tower.   **3.** Put the other stick through.

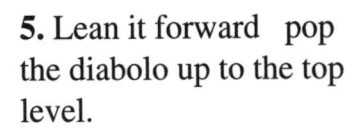

4. Spread the tower.

5. Lean it forward   pop the diabolo up to the top level.

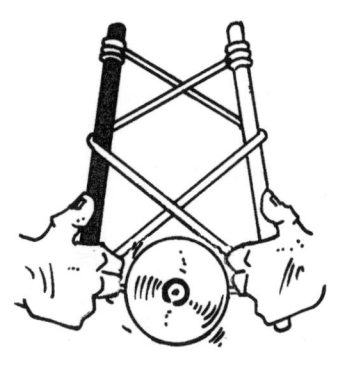 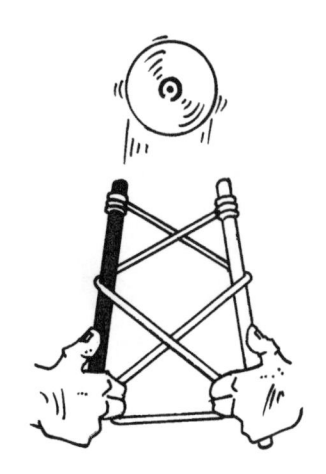

6. After you've shown it off (you'll hear the oohs and ahs), you can begin to collapse the tower.

7. First, release your fingertips and that will drop the diabolo down one floor (cradle position).

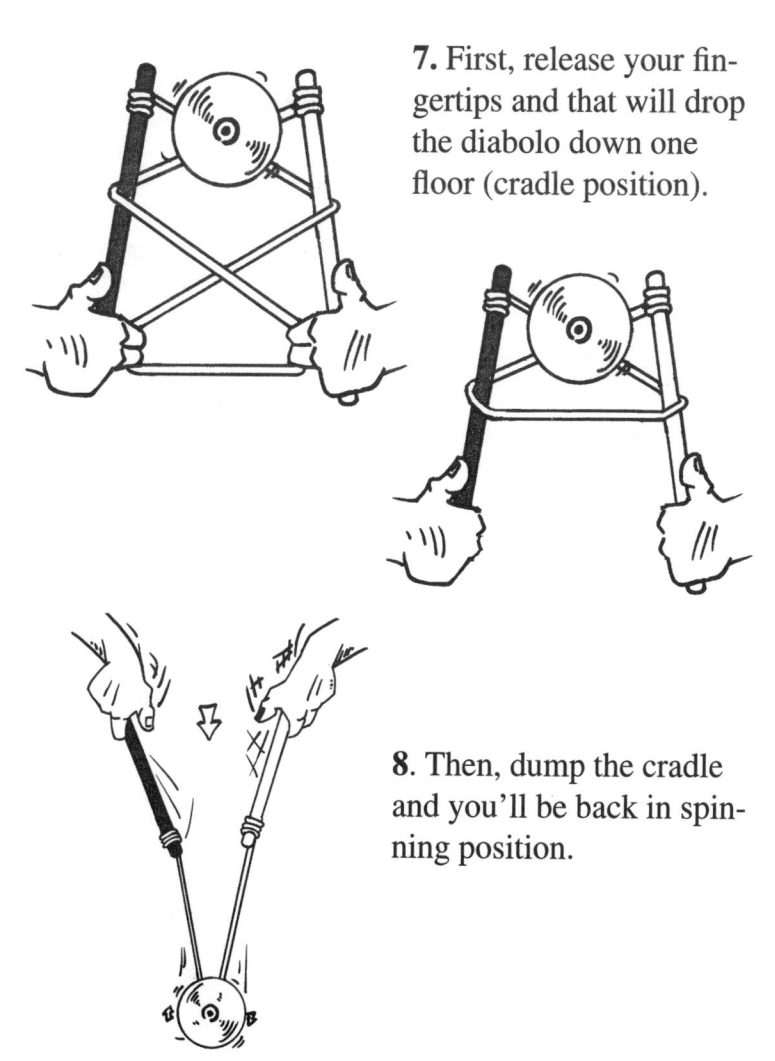

8. Then, dump the cradle and you'll be back in spinning position.

The Not

Here's a magic trick. It looks like a complex knot, but...uh...it's not. Again, start with lots of spin. Then, follow the illustrated steps:

1. Over

2. Under

3. Through

4. Over

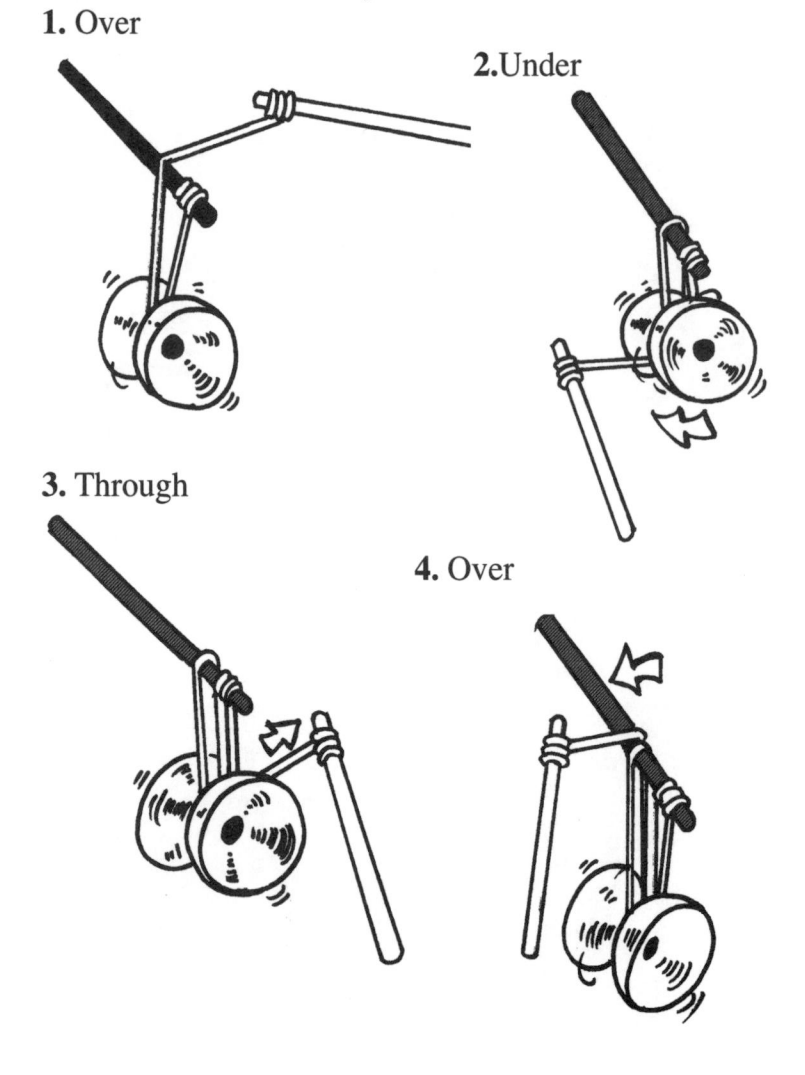

5. Under

6. Through...and then dump forward.

7. All that for nothing!

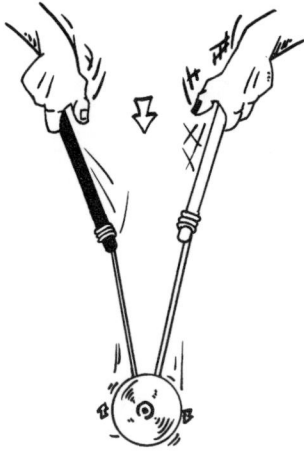

The easiest way to learn this trick is to have a friend hold the diabolo as you go through the sequence of moves. Then, spin it up and tie the not.

Advanced Orbits: Letting go

We talked about orbits earlier, but this section takes them one step more by introducing you to some real juggling variations in which you actually let go of the sticks and send them flying. We hope that you will catch them also.

One hand

Try this front orbit by sending it out to your non-accelerating side. Before you send it off however, move your accelerating stick up and perpendicular to the other. This is the overhead view from your perspective just before launch.

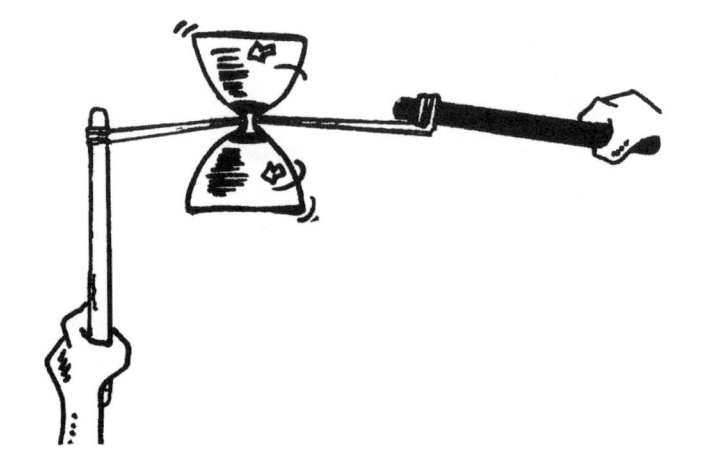

Now swing the orbit out and let go of the accelerating stick when the diabolo is almost to its highest point in the orbit. What happened?

If things are working right the loose stick should come flying right behind the

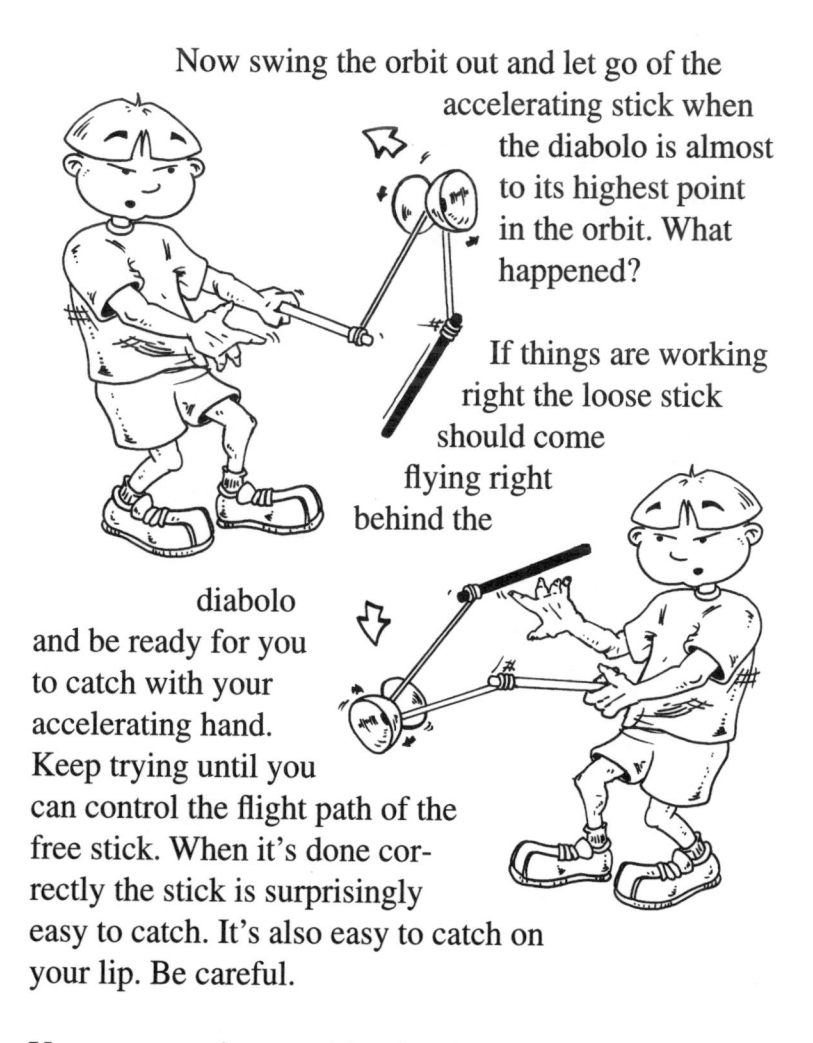

diabolo and be ready for you to catch with your accelerating hand. Keep trying until you can control the flight path of the free stick. When it's done correctly the stick is surprisingly easy to catch. It's also easy to catch on your lip. Be careful.

You can experiment with other flying stick moves. Almost any orbit will carry the stick over for you. Try under the leg and behind the back for starters.

67

Suicide

Got the one-handed orbit? OK, let's go for no hands!
It's suicide you say? Yes that's what we call it, but the
funny thing is that you feel fine if you do it right.

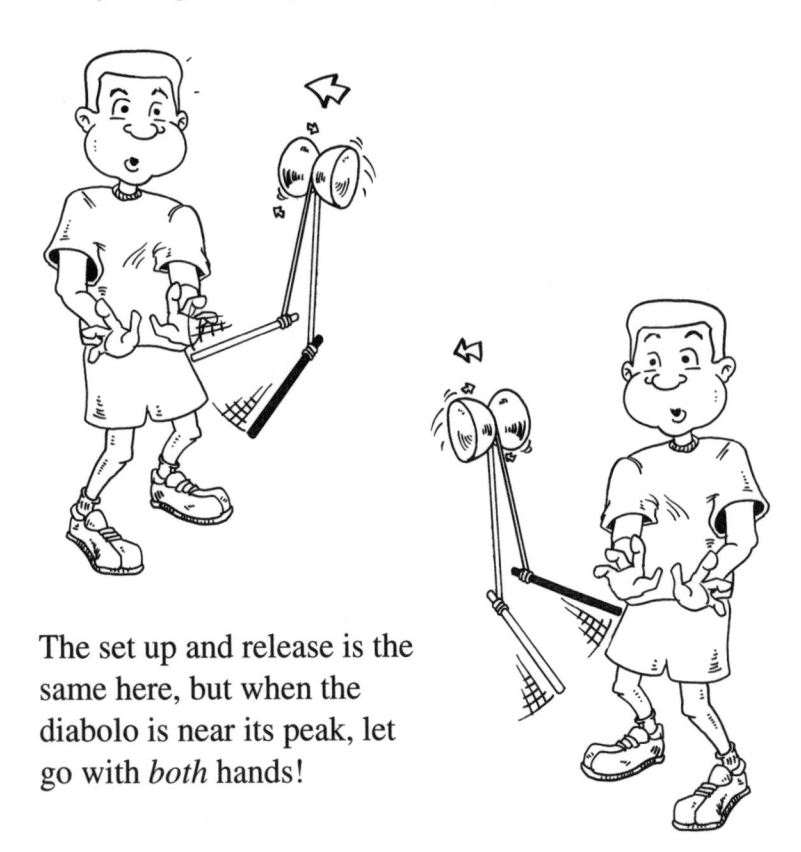

The set up and release is the
same here, but when the
diabolo is near its peak, let
go with *both* hands!

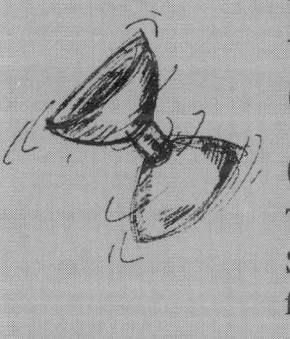

Proficiency Challenge

(Level 2-Jammer)

To achieve the Level 2 (Jammer) Skill Award, the candidate must fulfill the following:

A. Cross-Whipping

Using the cross-whipping method of acceleration, the candidate must be able to produce a smooth spin that is rapid enough to last at least 10 seconds after the cross-whipping motion is stopped.

Length of spin- _____ seconds

B. Circles

The candidate must demonstrate the ability to do a minimum of five each of the multiple circles listed below:

Front _____
Foot _____
Left leg ____
Right leg____
Alternating Right and left leg (5 each) _____
Arm____

69

C. Jumps

The candidate must demonstrate the ability to do a minimum of five each of the multiple jumps listed below:

Foot _____
Left leg _____
Right leg _____
Arm _____
Neck _____
Both arms _____

D. Advanced launches and catches, stick and string tricks and advanced orbits.

The candidate must demonstrate the ability to execute each the following skills in two consecutive attempts:

Launch with two rope skips and catch _____
Launch with spin or cartwheel to catch _____
Launch to cross-armed catch to opposite cross-armed catch _____
Launch to behind the back catch and launch to catch _____
Trampoline with a minimum of five bounces _____
Launch to whip catch with diabolo retaining spin_____

Stick grind for a minimum of five seconds to catch
with spin _____

Stick grind on one hand switched to other hand to catch
with spin _____
Stick grind carry under the leg to catch with spin ____
Stick grind carry behind the back to catch with spin

____
Elevator _____
Cradle back to spin _____
Eiffel Tower to spin _____
Not to spin _____
Front orbit with one released stick to catch _____
Under the leg or behind the back orbit with one
released stick to catch ____
Front orbit with two released sticks to catch _____

The candidate may make as many attempts at each
individual requirement as he or she desires, but the
entire challenge must be completed within a 60 minute
period.

The test results should be verified by two adult individuals who serve as examiners and timers. The examiners should initial each result and sign and date the completed application for certification.

Jester Games Diabolo Jammer Skill Award

Name_____

Address_____

_____

_____

Phone_____

E-mail_____

Has qualified in all the requirements for the Jammer
level of diabolo play as attested by:

_____

_____

This _____ day of _____, 19__

Mail complete test form and check or money order
(payable to Jester Games) for $12.00 to:

Jester Games
4924 Balboa #415
Encino, CA 91316
jestergames@hotmail.com

Certified players will receive a Jester Games Diabolo
Jammer Proficiency Certificate and a Jester Games hat.
Please allow 3 weeks for processing and mailing.

Continuity: Trick linking

So you've learned a lot of really cool tricks. That's great! The next step is to learn how to tie them all together. The very best players seem to move from one trick to another seamlessly. The best way to develop that style for yourself is to be thinking of how the end of one trick that you're working on may flow nicely into another trick that you like. After a while, if you concentrate on those transitions, you'll find that they become as smooth and natural to you as the sequence of songs on your favorite album. So don't just think... trick/trick/trick. Instead, think... play.

Co-ops: Partner play

Cooperative play is one of the most outstanding features of diabolo play. At the risk of dissing its little cousin the yo-yo too much, it is one of the diabolo's strongest advantages. Once you get the power launches and the catching down, diabolo play has all the movement and challenge of freestyle with a flying disc. Top players can zing a diabolo back and forth at amazing speed and over a great distance.

Face-to-face

If you haven't been working on both spins yet, now might be a good time to begin. When you're passing the diabolo from one person to another the spin direction becomes a major issue. If you and your playing partner prefer opposite spins then you'll want to toss to each other face-to-face. That way you'll each have the spin that you like.

Side-to-side

The key to an effective exchange is to make sure that your launch is smooth. Be sure that you have a good bit of spin and that the diabolo is not tilting when you launch. For face-to-face

exchanges, toss fairly high so that the diabolo will be coming down when it reaches your partner. For lower, faster exchanges it's better to set up side-to-side. That way you can more easily handle the forward motion of the diabolo. Keep the spin in mind. When players with opposite spins set up for side-to-side play they need to still be facing opposite directions. Same spin players will face the same direction.

Share the spin

Two or more players you can have a real jugglefest. Three diabolos between two players is a classic challenge. With more players, try different patterns that keep the diabolos moving. Again like freestyle disc play, the fun is in the creative launching and catching techniques. Try exchanges from stick grinds, cross-handed positions, under the leg, behind the back and from a trampoline series. There's no limit to the possibilities. Catching is even more exciting because it can be a real thrill to see a diabolo screaming down from the sky and nail it with a difficult catch. Try it, you'll get your daily requirement of adrenaline.

Multiple Diabolos: Juggle 'em!

When your tossing back and forth with your partner, you may want to use two diabolos. That way there's no waiting for action. Throw one and you've got one coming right back at you. For real thrills, try juggling three diabolos between the two of you. That should hold your attention.

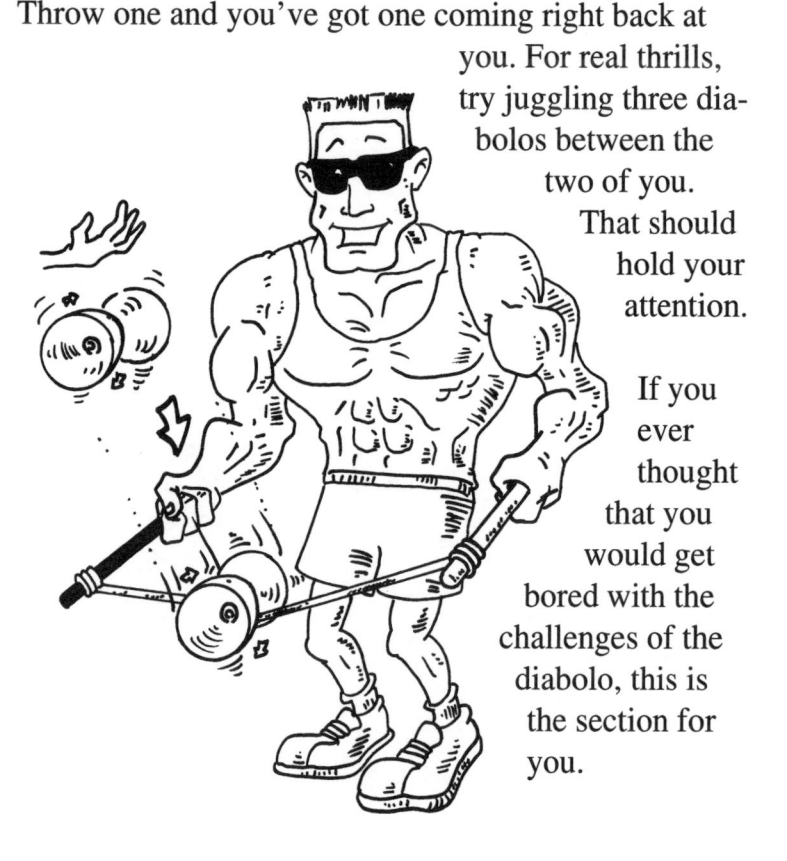

If you ever thought that you would get bored with the challenges of the diabolo, this is the section for you.

The first sure cure for overconfidence is to try spinning multiple diabolos yourself. Yes, at the same time! There are talented players who can actually manage four at once! Don't worry about that for a while. Just spinning two should keep you off the streets for quite a while.

The easiest way to get started with two diabolos is to have one going in a front circle and then have a partner either toss you a second one or place a second one on your string. In either case, the second diabolo should enter your circle on the accelerating stick side.

When the second diabolo comes into play it will bounce the string. What really happens is that you will be jumping each diabolo over the other in a circular motion. Once you get the rhythm going you'll find that the two follow each other through the circle like magic. To keep that magic going you'll have to learn to adjust for tipping and turning just as you did for a single diabolo.

If you think this is only twice as difficult to do with two, you don't understand the situation. Each one is *geometrically* harder (that's a lot). You have to make the separate adjustments for each diabolo by tapping them with your accelerating stick. It's more of an art than a science, but it's still physics.

Almost all of the single diabolo moves can be done with two or three also. You're definitely ready for the big time when you can do many different tricks with three. At that point you may begin to think about the possibility of four. Four is flat-out awesome. Send us your video, dude!

Skill Games

There are a number of skill tests in the Jester Games proficiency standards for diabolo. Some of these become routine for advanced players. Counting the number of leg circles that you can do in a row will become an endurance and computation challenge. There are skill games that continue to be fun however especially if you have other players to provide some competition.

MTA/ TRC

Maximum time aloft and throw run and catch are both challenglng and fun. In MTA, start a stopwatch at the instant of release and stop it on first contact of a successful spinning catch. TRC is measured from the point of the throw to the point of the catch. You have to be a good thrower and runner to get a good distance.

Tennis

There have been several periods of history in which diabolo tennis was very popular. You can try it on badminton or volleyball courts that have high nets. If you use a tennis court, play in the backcourt area. The diabolo must be thrown level with spin and land in the opponent's court to be good. You will really begin to see the advantages of knowing both spins!

Proficiency Challenge
(Level 3-Master)

The Master proficiency level is reserved for players who have achieved the Spinner and Jammer level and have also demonstrated additional mastery. This includes a high level of artistic virtuosity, athletic mastery and teaching competency.

Application for consideration is arranged on an individual basis and includes submission of a freestyle tape and a playing resume and letters of recommendation from fellow players and students.

Interested candidates who have passed the Spinner and Jammer levels may inquire about consideration for the Master proficiency level by contacting:

Jester Games
4924 Balboa #415
Encino, CA 91316
jestergames@hotmail.com

The vision: see and share

In the course of discovering the challenges of the diabolo, we trust that you have also come to realize what a wonderful opportunity it offers. It promises the satisfaction that comes both from the mastery of skills and from the tantalizing promise of more to be learned. Its play can keep us physically and mentally agile over the course of a lifetime. And perhaps most importantly, it also offers us the gift of humility. We hope you will use all of these opportunities to the fullest and that you will enrich the lives of those around you.

A few words from the head Jester

My love affair with the diabolo began when a friend showed me one in France around 1990. At the time I was passing my Ultra Light Airplane pilot's license and I was thinking about developing some ULM tours in Africa. Little did I know then that I would come to the United States and manufacture my own diabolo instead.

When I first played, nobody explained to me how to do it and of course I had no book. It was just my diabolo and me. Figure it out! Well, with the help of some friends, we did. Progress was slow but the fun and addiction was there. Soon we were a little group playing near the lake, at the park, in town, concerts, at home, in short...everywhere!

Not long after that, four of us decided to go sell some diabolos in the south of France. It was a great experience. We were doing shows and we sold a lot on the beach, mostly in little towns. During that time we taught thousands of people how to play. And I learned a lot about what made a good diabolo.

The one we were selling was fairly good quality, but it retailed for $40, which was too expensive for a lot of people. After this summer, I traveled around the world with a backpack and of course the diabolos, which allowed me to meet great people and stop at the Club Med resorts in Bali and Guadeloupe for shows and a grand tour in the Caribbean night clubs!

What I discovered in my travels was that even though the diabolo was ancient, it was virtually unknown in many parts of the world. I also found that the diabolo never failed to intrigue and enchant almost everyone of any age. After the first fear of looking ridiculous trying it, people then realized that it is in fact easy to learn, and great fun to become more and more skilled. The question that people always seemed to ask was, "Where can I get one?"

After hearing that many times, I decided that one of the best places in the world to sell the diabolo would be in Venice Beach, California. So I came here and designed my own Diabolo with the best size, weight and material possible. I also was able to make it available for a price that almost anyone can afford. At first it didn't come out perfectly, but after almost two years of work and testing, it finally did. The Jester Games Diabolo was born!

Venice Beach turned out to not the best place to sell the diabolo after all. At least not to start diabolo mania like it is in Europe. For that I needed to find a way to make the Diabolo known to many more people.

At that point, I met this cool guy named Scott Cleere from Creative Athletics. It turned out that he was a footbag champion who had developed a business doing school tours with others cool games like the diabolo. After a couple of years in Scott's school programs, the diabolo started to become well known enough for the next move which was to begin selling it in stores. That's when I met Steven Poreda (an amazing devil sticks player) and Arlene from Infinity, Inc. They manufacture the Mystix and also became distributors of the Jester Games diabolo. So with their help, and the help of a cool diabolo video made by James De Oliviera (who is also a great juggling performer and diabolo enthusiast), you can now find the Jester Games diabolo in the finest toy and specialty stores.

But there still was something missing. People who bought the Jester Games diabolo, didn't realize all the wonderful things they could do with it. We needed a book and more programs to help players learn. That's when I met Dan "The Stork" Roddick who joined the Jesters team in 1998. He wrote and edited this book and is helping us develop many other exciting projects to spread the word about the diabolo. Stork (a former world champion of flying disc freestyle) is a game designer and promoter and he has been one of the key people who have developed flying disc play over the last 30 years. To make the book even more useful and fun, we got the help of Mike Daley. Mike is a hot footbag player and as you can see, a talented artist with a great eye for capturing action. So we put all that talent together in this little book just for you! We hope you'll have as much fun with your diabolo as we have had and that you'll share it with your friends too.